Beth Gets a Snack

by Trisha Roberts
illustrated by Shawn McManus

Core Decodable 41

McGraw Hill Education

Bothell, WA • Chicago, IL • Columbus, OH • New York, NY

MHEonline.com

Send all inquiries to:
McGraw-Hill Education
8787 Orion Place
Columbus, OH 43240

ISBN: 978-0-02-145391-7
MHID: 0-02-145391-8

Printed in Canada.

9 10 11 12 KOD 24

Beth is a thin bug.
Can Beth have a snack?

Is fabric a snack?

Beth can get fabric.

This is Seth.

Seth gets a bath.

Seth has a bedspread.
That bedspread has thick threads.

Beth is thrilled!

Seth's bedspread is a snack.

Beth is not thin.

Thick thread is in Beth!